ईप्सा

पा लेने की इच्छा के क्षितिज से कहीं नीचे और खो
देने के भय की सतह से कहीं ऊपर

Akash Anurag

BookLeaf Publishing
India | USA | UK

Made with ❤ on the BookLeaf Publishing Platform
www.bookleafpub.in
www.bookleafpub.com

Dedication

To Baba*.... for making me fall in love with literature.*

To Maa*..... you are a river that deposited the sediments for what I am today.*

To Cocu - The Muse *of all my blabberings that can be called poetry..... - Thank you for standing up to me and telling me, do not write to please me. Till it does not come from within, do not write. Write a book and without the fear that no one will ever read it, because you deserve to do it for yourself.* **Any form of my writing or creativity will always draw its inspiration from you. You are that river which liberated this collection of sediments from many of its own fears and nudged it towards journeys it always wanted to trudge on but lacked the heart to start.**

Preface

I had never wanted to write a book containing poems. I had never wanted to write any kind of book. But to be very honest, I had always dreamt of my name being there on a book cover. Alas, the hypocrisy of being human. The fear of writing a book always stemmed from the fear of it being criticised and the greater fear of not being read by anyone.

Very rarely in a poet's/ writer's or any creative person's life, I love to think that I am a bit creative, comes around a muse. When you find one, you also find liberation from a lot of your erstwhile fears. This book is a result of a series of conversations which started with "you should compile your poems or what you write in the form of a book", building to the liberation of " You must write. If you do not, you will be doing a great disservice to yourself. And why do you fear that no one will read it. Why do you need that validation? If you ever write a book, you will always have one reader,and that will be me". And that is how a conversation at the beach finally liberated me from this fear of validation.

It's not necessarily true that muses become a part of your life, too. Not always, but in a sense, they do, because they inspire your art and influence your artistic output, for when you think and pen or even when your thoughts flow, you can't exclude them from your thoughts. Mine, not only liberated me from the fear as mentioned above, but also shaped my poems. Like a river that crafts deposited sediments, her crafting of my thoughts is writ large on most poems here, and I am ever thankful to her for this. Thus, this book is an outcome of love, not a desire to possess, inspired by my days and conversations with someone who inspires my thoughts

Acknowledgements

I am very thankful to the publishers for being so warm and helpful towards me in the first place. I can not imagine finishing this book amid my failing health without their support and insights. Since, almost no one knows about the fact that I undertook writing this, I am still very thankful to my friends, family, ***Adya*** and off course ***"Cocu"*** for all their support and at times pushing me in a certain direction to bring me out of my comfort zone and most importantly, for not giving up on me when I was close to doing so on many ocassions. A token of thanks goes out to ***Aakanksha*** for allowing me to use her work as the cover design for the book.

Last but not least, thank you, Bhagwati, for all the strength.

1. Dependence

They say that love is complicated,
But love and loving are not but it is people who are complicated,
My love for you is simple,
Listen patiently, woman with that beautiful dimple.

It is in saying Goodnight to be read as I Love You every night,
It is in being there by each other's side conquering every fright,
It is in every text me when you reach and it is in learning and adapting
with every lesson that has life has to teach.
It is in finding unlimited happiness in each other's minimum bare,
And it is in the assurance that come what may I will be there,
It is in making days out of a date,
And mostly it is in "I will wait" while taking nobody's bait.

It is in listening without a word,
It is in creating memories against time's sword,
It is in those "this book reminds me of you",

It is in in watching those light from Elliot's go ***Bhook Bhaak Bhoo***.

Maybe it is also in trying to understand how each of us feel,
Or maybe it is in the realisation that that with each other we are more real.

Mind you, all love is effortless but yet an effort,
I know of countless nights when you type a text and resist,
You know of days when I want to say something but I desist,
Life is difficult, love does not need to be,
We fight our own battles alone with independence,
But the dependence of leaning on one another is beautiful too, you see.

2. Aam Aadmi Kehlata Hoon.

मेरी सुबह शुरू होती है अखबार के साथ,
कुछ खबरें पढ़ कर अंदर ही अंदर उबल जाता हूँ,
पर फिर अपने मन को समझाता हूँ और मंद पर जाता हूँ,
मैं एक आम आदमी कहलाता हूँ।

फिर निकलता हूँ अपने दफ्तर,
कभी मेट्रो तो कभी बसों के धक्के खाता हूँ,
सोचता हूँ एक गाडी ले ही लूँ,
लेकिन फिर अपनों के जरूरतों की सोच कर,
अपने इक्छाओं को समझाता हूँ,
मैं एक आम आदमी कहलाता हूँ।

फिर जाता हूँ राशन की दुकानों पर,
कतारों में खड़ा रह कर अपने घर कुछ सामन लाता हूँ,
उस थोड़े से सामान मैं से कुछ सामान अपने बच्चों के बीच में बाँट कर,
उनकी हंसी में अपनी खुशियां शायद पा जाता हूँ,
कैसे समझाऊँ उन्हें मैं की हर रोज़ महंगाई और मर अपने खो चुके सपनों से एक जंग लड़ता हूँ,
और हर रोज़ शायद हार जाता हूँ,
पर फिर भी उनकी मुस्कान खुश रहने की कोशिश करता हूँ,
और बाकी सब भूल जाता हूँ,
मैं एक आम आदमी कहलाता हूँ।

दफ्तर मैं रोज़ बॉस के ताने खाता हूँ,
मन कुंठित तो होता है मेरा,
पर अपनों की सोच फिर से काम मैं लग जाता हूँ,
हर छब्बीस जनवरी और पंद्रह अगस्त को देशभक्ति की गीत जाता हूँ,
और अगले ही दिन बहुत सारे नियमों की धज्जियाँ उडाता हूँ,
थोड़ा शर्माता हूँ और फिर उस शर्म को भूल जाता हूँ,
मैं एक आम आदमी कहलाता हूँ ।

ऐसा नहीं है की सोचता नहीं हूँ मैं,
रात को अपनी तन्हाई से जब गुफ्तगु करता हूँ तो पूछ लेता हूँ,
की आखिर क्या वजूद है मेरा ?
क्या बस मैं जितने पैसे कमाता हूँ वही मेरी पहचान है ?
सब कुछ छोड़ कर गायब हो जाने में ही शायद मेरी शांति थी और है,
पर अगले ही मन अपनों की शक्ल याद कर,
मन को बोलता हूँ "यार छोडो कल ऑफिस भी तो जाना है",
और चद्दर तान सो जाता हूँ,
इसलिए शायद एक आम आदमी कहलाता हूँ।

3. Kaun ho? Kya Ho?

तुम क्या हो और कौन हो ?
शायद तुम वो इठलाती वसंत हो और मैं निर्जीव पतझड़,
शायद तुम हो उस आसमान का चमकता सितारा और मैं टूटता तारा,
शायद तुम हो वो सुन्दर कविता हो और मैं एक निशब्द,
नाकामयाब शायर ,
जिसके शब्द कहना तो बोहोत कुछ चाहते हैं पर न जाने क्यों दिल है
कायर......

तुम वो सुन्दर सपना हो जिसे मेरी नींद चाहे की वो अपना हो ,
खैर क्या करूँ, मैं तो बिना नींदों की रातों सरीखा हूँ,
तुम हो एक बेमिसाल पर एक जटिल सवाल और शायद मैं और मेरी
कवितायेँ उंनका जवाब,
तुम शायद मेरे सब कुछ हो और मैं शायद तुम्हारा कुछ भी नहीं,
या मैं तुम्हारा कुछ हूँ और तुम मेरे बोहोत कुछ,
पर जो भी हो और जैसी भी हो पर मेरी कविताओं में तो सबसे सुन्दर,
अपने हर ऐब के साथ, तुम मेरी हो.....

4. You and the Sea

As I sit by the sea thinking about Madras and Tomorrow,
Pondering as to how much of your time I would like to borrow,
The time that I would want to turn and live like a lifetime,
Before it runs out and it's time yet again for goodbyes,
The wait till I get to be hypnotised by every motion of those beautiful eyes,
God Damn! Why does time fly?

Clinging to these thoughts as my eyes look yonder,
I can not help but profusely wander,
How much are you and the sea similar?
Wondering, whether you are with these thoughts familiar?
You calm me down in the tempest of storms like the sea,
Your importance in my existence, you being so integral to my being, something only for you to feel and see.

Well, the similarities or what I see as identical do not end there,
The resemblances are here, there and everywhere,
Your eyes have the depth of the ocean with their calmness often masking the millions of mutinies and

storms that brew inside of you,
Just like the sea, often so rebellious yet calm,
A sense of energy and exuberance marks you both,
The way you move reminds of the vigour of the sea,
cherubic yet sturdy - a juxtaposition unique henceforth,
Both of you have the depth of your hearts along with
which the largeness of it follows hand-in-hand,
The depth from which you draw the strength to fight it
all,
And also the strength to forgive me and all my falls.

There are days when it is the sea that I envy,
For it has the memory chest of all your days, both happy
and dreary,
With the sea, you have piggy banked many of your
feelings and stories,
In its waves are stored the many tales of you that I don't
know of, of the darkness you've fought and your glories,
And though it also reminds me of all those times when I
should have been there for you and could not be,
Yet I am thankful that the sea was there and so was that
magical window overlooking that eucalyptus tree.

I have often dreamt of sitting with you for hours by the
Auroville Beach,
Listening to you, never wanting you to stop, while time
pauses and the waves screech,

As I look at your cascading gossamer of black with awe,
waving like the waves,
Free and unwavering like your beautiful soul intact, the
happiness of which is what the "I" in me truly craves.

5. The Healing of a Beautiful Soul

How could she have known that ***she was a bit lost***
without having first wondered?
Getting lost is but natural, not an anomaly that should leave her bewildered.
Why should she keep herself at bay?
When she is a river, which is meant to flow and find its way.
How would she know that maybe her pursuit of certain goals was but a futility ?,
Had she not gone after them, ignoring all conceptions and notions of utility.

Sometimes, in order to be whole, ***you have to be incomplete first,***
It is like the love a traveller has for sources of water, after a long, sustained thirst,
Her dreams and aspirations will definitely take flight,
When finally crosses the tunnel, her unflinching light,
For even in the darkness of times, she has never learnt to give up on herself and her fight.

Maybe yes, that is what it is like to be whole,
The healing of a beautiful soul.

6. Ye Jo Nain Tumhare Hain....

ये जो नैन तुम्हारे हैं,
इस स्याह रात से भी कारे हैं,
झाँकूँ जब भी इनमें, मुझे दिखते अफ़साने कई सारे हैं,
ये जो नैन तुम्हारे हैं,
इस स्याह रात से भी कारे हैं.....

ये जो नैन तुम्हारे हैं,
राज़ तुम्हारे समेटे इन्होने सारे हैं,
बिना तुम्हारे कुछ बोले भी तुम्हारे हर भाव को उकेरे हैं,
समझो ना की तुम्हारे अंधेरों में भी सवेरे हैं,
ये जो नैन तुम्हारे हैं,
इस रात की नफासत से भी न्यारे हैं....

ये जो नैन तुम्हारे हैं,
अनजाने मैं ही दिल इन पर हम बार बार हरे हैं,
शायद इल्हाम ना हो तुम्हें पर ये बस आँखें नहीं रुखसार हैं,
हारी और वारि जिन पर हमारी कलम बार बार है,
ये जो नैन तुम्हारे हैं,
इस स्याह रात की गहराइयों से भी कारे हैं......

ये जो नैन तुम्हारे हैं,
क्या नाम इनके कई सारे हैं ?
मृगनयनी कहूँ तुम्हें या कहूँ कामाक्षी,

मदद करो मेरी थोड़ी तुम भी,
ये जो नैन तुम्हारे हैं,
इनके समक्ष शब्द भी मेरे सम्मोहित हैं, हारे हैं.....

ये जो नैन तुम्हारे हैं,
कुछ कुछ बंदिशशुदा पर फिर भी ना जाने कैसे आज़ाद और आवारे हैं
,
बिलकुल तुम्हारी तरह अपनी रूह रूह से सजदेदार पर फिर भी
बंजारे हैं,
ये जो नैन तुम्हारे हैं....

खूबसूरत हैं ये इतने की शब्द कम मेरे पड़ जाएँ,
इनकी कहानी मेरी ये सस्ती शायरी भी बयां ना कर पाए,
कुछ तो हम भी हैं नाकारा और कुछ इन नैनों की मतवालियाँ इतनी
की शायद वक़्त ही कम पड़ जाए,
आकांक्षा है बस इतनी की तौसीफ में इनकी उम्र भर लिखता रहूँ
आयतें,
शायद ये रह जाएँ बन कर हमारे दरम्यान की रिवायतें....

ये जो नैन तुम्हारे हैं.....

7. Footnote

When your story is written,
With countless tales of courage and grit smitten,
I know that I might not even attract a chapter,
For it's your story of triumph amidst disaster.

But then sometimes I wonder,
As my mind strolls and ponders,
Will I even be a paragraph?
Or maybe a blip on your growth graph.

Through the highs and the lows sails your boat,
I know that in that story of yours I will be a footnote,
Which the readers of the story won't even glance at, forget dote,
But the footnotes are still a part of the story that you wrote.

For casual readers, the footnote is just an insignificant dot,
But for the one who wrote the story its significance is not lost,
For footnotes are silent pillars of support,
On whom you can rest and fall back without the fear of questions or any retort.

A footnote does not ask for recognition or any tags of societal validation,
For in its writer's happiness and comfort lies its utmost elation,
Though nobody notices yet it does not remain unnoticed,
It loves its existence as a silent safe space, ignored by non-relevant readers yet relevant.

At the end of days, maybe this is the point of it all,
To be there to hold you and push you to get up every time that you fall,
In a world where the race for validation and being a main character in your story may be a fling,
Being that footnote in your story which only you can see, is perhaps the whole point of this, the most beautiful thing.

When your story is written by you,
I may not be a chapter or a paragraph for people to notice,
For being that footnote is perhaps the only motive.....

8. When it is over

I know that you have read Mary Oliver,
And I know that you are a firm believer,
That I will know when it is over,
But then, when and what will get over?

Will your scent over my shirt after you have left, fade?
Or will the feeling that you are just around when I try to paint you wane?
Or will the fact that I am reminded of your hair every time that I am staring at a rippling cascade?
If all these were mere infatuations and not love, they would not have stayed.

So then, when and what will get over?
It often perturbs my mind as it sets to hover,
Maybe I rushed it all when I should have been slower,
But then I am human and I am not bound to never make mistakes ever.

How and when does it get over?
Every time I picture you while reading Harry Potter,
There is but that smile, still on my face every night, and the other,
When I sleep, to your voice saying, "I shaw an otter".

Maybe even when it is over, I may still not know,
For love is sensible yet foolish in all its ebbs and flows,
It is like sculpting a garden, waiting for flowers with
seeds of trust and innocence that you sow,
Surely one moves over relationships, but then you are
love, and moving over love is something that I will never
know.

Probably when it is even over, I will never know,
Alive I have been for long, but lived I have only once,
For a love like you comes but only like a chance,
I would live with your scent and your memories rather
than letting them go at a glance,
For those are the only moments when this heart
experienced romance,
So letting them go would be a death blow,
If and when it is over, I probably do not want to know.

9. The Beauty of a Flower

The beauty of a flower,
Amidst all of life's sunshine and showers,
Is not in it being delicate,
But in the stubbornness of its will to grow,
Despite at times that growth being slow.

The journey of the flower is not easy,
There are periods of ups and downs,
At times, there are questions on its journey and the occasional frowns,
But the flower still grows for it has the will to grow,
The world at times tried to bend it, but has the flower ever learnt how to bow?

Mind you, the journey of a flower is not easy,
It is not at all times hunky dory, sunshine and cheesy,
It falls to the ground, it is plucked, there are struggles inside in which its torn,
Do not be fooled by its cheerful exterior, for there are wounds it has silently worn,
For every time it falls to the ground, like a phoenix, it rises,
Nourishing the same tree it fell from, restarting its journey as it once again strives and blooms.

You are that flower,
Do not forget it amidst all hail and shower,
Your journey is your own, fast or slow,
You are beautiful, the core of it lies in your will to grow,
For your beauty, dear flower,
Amidst all of life's sunshine and showers,
Is not in you to be merely delicate,
But in the stubbornness of your will to grow,
Amidst all of life's ebb and flow.

10. हाँ, मैं तुमसे प्रेम करता हूँ......

हाँ मैं तुमसे प्रेम करता हूँ,
ठीक उस तरह जैसे मछलियां पानी से करती हैं,
धमनियां रक्त से करती हैं,
पौधे फूलों से करते हैं,
और गर्मी से तपती ज़मीं बारिश की बूंदों से करती है।

हाँ मैं तुमसे प्रेम करता हूँ,
पर उस तरह नहीं जैसे भँवरे फूलों से करते हैं,
उस तरह भी नहीं जैसे शमा मोम से करती है,
या प्रकार भी नहीं जैसे पतंगे रौशनी से करते हैं,
मैं इन प्रकारों से तुमसे प्रेम नहीं करता पर हाँ मैं तुमसे प्रेम करता हूँ।

हाँ मैं तुमसे प्रेम करता हूँ,
शायद उस तरह से जैसे नींद सपनों से करती है,
और आखें नींद से,
थोड़ा उस प्रकार भी जैसे स्याही कलम से करती है,
और कलम कागज़ से,
हाँ मैं तुमसे कई और प्रकारों से प्रेम करता हूँ और कई और प्रकारों से नहीं भी,
हाँ मैं तुमसे प्रेम करता हूँ।

हाँ मैं तुमसे प्रेम करता हूँ ,
और मैं प्रेम बस तुम्हारे शरीर से नहीं बल्कि तुम्हारे अंदर के उस स्वयं

और उसके अंदर के उस बचपन से भी करता हूँ,
वो बचपन जिसे तुम इस दुनिया की क्रूर धुप से अपनी छाँव मैं बचने की हर कोशिश करती हो,
मैं कोशिश करता हूँ की तुम्हारे रंग और स्वरुप मैं प्रेम कर सकूं,
अक्सर असफल रहता हूँ, गलतियां करता हूँ अपनी कोशिहों मैं,
लेकिन डरता नहीं हूँ क्यूंकि तुम मुझे जानती हो, समझती हो,
क्यूंकि तुम मुझे समझती हो इसलिए माफ़ भी कर सकने की क्षमता रखती हो।

हाँ मैं तुमसे प्रेम करता हूँ ,
मैं जानता हूँ की तुम पूछोगी मुझसे या फिर खुद से की ,
क्यों मैं कुछ प्रकारों से तुम्हें प्रेम करता हूँ और कई प्रकारों से नहीं ?
जिन प्रकारों से मैं प्रेम करता हूँ तुमसे उनमें मुझे बस पा लेने भर की लालसा नहीं दिखती ,
ऐसा नहीं है की मेरी इक्छा नहीं है
की तुम मेरे जीवन का वो हिस्सा बनो जो सदैव के लिए रहे ,
मेरी इस कहानी का वो किस्सा बनो जिसे हम दोनों कभी लिखना न बंद करे ,
पर तुम्हें बस पा लेने की इक्छा और तुमसे कुछ ले लेने की अभिलाषा के क्षितिज के नीचे मेरा वो प्रेम बस्ता है ,
जिससे मैं बोहोत प्रेम करता हूँ।

हाँ मैं तुमसे प्रेम करता हूँ ,
और ये प्रेम मुझे निडर बनता है ,
और कभी कभी भयभीत भी करता है की कहीं खो न दूँ तुम्हें ,
पर खो देने किस इस भय इक इस धरातल से कहीं ऊपर मेरे प्रेम बस्ता है ,

शायद इसलिए इस भय के बावजूद मैं तुमसे प्रेम करता हूँ।

अगर गौर से देखा जाये ,
तो शायद मैं कभी भी न पूरा बतला पाऊँगा की मैं तुमसे प्रेम क्यों कर ता हूँ ,
और मैं चाहता भी नहीं को पूरा बतला पाऊं ,
इसी बहाने ता उम्र कोशिश तो नहीं छोड़ूंगा ,
पर इतना तो पूर्णतः बतला ही सकता हूँ की तुम्हें पा लेने की इक्छा के क्षितिज के कहीं नीचे ,
और तुम्हें खो देने के भय के धरातल के कहीं ऊपर,
एक जगह है , वहीँ बस्ता है मेरा प्रेम तुम्हारे लिए ।

हाँ मैं तुमसे प्रेम करता हूँ ,
और मैं बस इतना चाहता हूँ की एक दिन तुम भी कहो की ,
हाँ मैं तुमसे प्रेम करती हूँ ,
और उस प्रेम से प्रेम करती हूँ अपने प्रकारों से।

11. Rippling Cascades

Like a rippling cascade of immortality, it descends,
Down the glowing skin of her neck,
A cascade of beauty, a cascade of immortality,
A cascade full of black glowing waters,
Amidst the glowing, beauteous halo of the only deity I have ever known.

Her hair has the same delicacy as that of gossamer,
When it ripples in the wind, it makes me go mad,
It sends chills down my arms, for it makes me wonder and imagine,
Is that the paradise I have been seeking and longing for all my life?
When I see them, the first thought that crops up is that let me get lost in them,
For they are the worthiest items of beauty my eyes will ever behold.

Your hair is an ocean of unfathomable elegance,
An ocean in which I would love to be drowned any day,
Have you even tried to listen to the voice of the immortal waters which gush down your fountains ?
It boasts a mixture of beauty and depth,
Of a fountain of vigour, a fountain of youth.

Those locks in your hair, they steal my heart,
Whenever I see them around, my world goes upside down,
But you know your hair, just like you, is a youthful spirit released at last,
Narrow like a river at its source,
Yet like the oceans in its eternity, profound and vast.

12. T Gate

Every 4th Saturday night at eight,
When you step out of the T Gate,
Your Eyes would be met with a familiar sight on every date,
Of someone standing there, patiently in wait,
Outside the T Gate.

Do not be perturbed by his presence,
For he does not know how to make you feel his absence,
He loves the feel of waiting for you, as if though the most fateful part of his fate,
Like a swan waits without complaints, waiting happily for its mate
All of this and much more outside the Tharamani Gate.

T Gate is much more and not just a gate,
It has seen tears, hopes, goodbyes, and feelings evolve and oscillate,
Standing there like a border,
At which our words have often lost their order,
Its trees have seen our eyes speak and our blabberings run short and shorter,
Watching over, as the distance between us shrinks and grows no broader.

Extraordinary people might not find it remarkable,
But for two normal people, it is in its ways of its own, spectacular,
It marks the spot at which someone always waits for someone to turn,
It is also where, after you have disappeared, my tears do not know yet how not to run,
It is the silent gatekeeper to your golden memories, a task at which it shall not fail,
Hoard and hold them closer because with time for my sense of memory might eventually pale.

Magic happens, and sometimes at ordinary places,
In words left unspoken and yet spoken in glances,
How can anyone else appreciate the beauty of it, what are the chances?
Only Tharamani knows that you are the cloud which when pours, it rains,
Only Tharamani understands that I am that Aashadh ka Baadal which wants to express but it knows not how to rain,
Would not this magic wane if we stop trusting our hearts and trusted only our brains?

O, T Gate, you shall always be dear,
In this mazy life, you and waiting by your trees are the

only things that are clear,
You taught me why all patience does not mean an eternal wait.
Every Sunday morning at eight,
When with a heavy but happy heart he drops you at the Tharamani Gate,
Time stops for him, but then your memories do not obliterate,
They only add up as to himself, he says, "Go get them, I am here and I shall wait",
Believing in you, while arranging your memories on his memory chip plate,
Not paying heed to anything that is said about you, for I won't fall for the world's bait,
Waiting happily at the T Gate......

13. आकांक्षाएं और इक्छाएं ......

तुम्हारी कुछ आकांक्षाएं हैं,
मेरी कुछ इक्छाएं हैं,
पर ये ज़रूरी तो नहीं की इनके बीच हमेशा एक संघर्ष हो ?

तुम्हारी आकांक्षा है की तुम एक आज़ाद पंछी की तरह उस आकाश में उड़ो,
मेरे इक्छा है की तुम हर आकाश के क्षितिज को छुओ, पर जब थक जाओ,
तो वापस लौट के आओ इसी वृक्ष पर जो तुम्हारे इंतज़ार की आस लगाए रहता है।

तुम्हारी कुछ आकांक्षाएं बेहद छोटी, पर प्यारी हैं ,
जैसे की तुम्हें कोई प्यार करे, समझे, उसके लिए जो तुम हो,
और न उसके लिए जैसा की वो चाहता है की तुम बनो,
मेरी इक्छा है की मैं तुम्हारी इस कहानी का एक भाग बनूँ,
तुम्हारे हर आकर और प्रकार से प्रेम करूँ और करना सीख सकूं,
बिना इस अभिलाषा के की तुम मेरी हर इक्छा को पूरी करो ।

तुम्हारी आकांक्षा है की कोई तुम्हारे साथ चले, कोई तुम्हरी इस लड़ाई में हमेशा साथ रहे ,
मेरी इक्छा है की कोई तो ऐसा हो जिसके साथ मीलों चलूँ तो भी काम लगे,
कोई तो ऐसा हो जिसके लिए मैं भी लड़ूँ, जिसके ऊपर कभी भी विष्वास करना काम न करूँ,

अगर देखो गौर से तो बहुत छोटी इक्छाएं और आकांक्षाएं हैं मेरी तुम्हारी,
अगर न देखो तो बहुत बड़ी इक्छाएं और आकांक्षाएं हैं मेरी तुम्हारी,
पर क्यूंकि मैं और तुम एक दुसरे को बोहोत सच्ची से देखते हैं तो ये पता है हमें की शायद छोटी से ही आकांक्षाएं हैं मेरी तेरी।

क्या ये खुद में खूबसूरत नहीं है की मेरी इकचायें चाहती हैं की तुम्हारी हर आकांक्षा की पूर्ती हो,
और तुम्हारी आकांक्षाएं ये चाहती हैं की मेरी भी वो हर इक्छा पूरी हूँ जो वो कर सकती हैं ,
बिना इस दवाब की उन्हें उन्हें पूरा करना ही है,
क्या ये खुद में खूबसूरत नहीं है,
क्या यही वो मासूम co - dependence नहीं है जिसकी तुम बात करती हो ?

क्या ये खुद में खूबसूरत नहीं है की मेरी इक्छाएं बल दें तुम्हारी आकांक्षाओं को और तुम्हारी आकांक्षाएं उम्मीद दें मेरी इक्छाओं को,
सोचो तो इतना जटिल भी नहीं है ज़िन्दगी और बोहोत सोचो तो काफी जटिल भी है,
पर क्या फायदा अगर हम दोनों सोचते ही रह जाये और जीना ही भूल जाएं,
केवल हानि ही है अगर एक दोनों की लिए यादें ही बनाना बिसर जाएं।

तुम्हारी कुछ आकांक्षाओं में से एक हैं की तुम खुश रहो,
मेरी आखिरी इक्छा की भाँती पहली इक्छा है तुम्हारी ख़ुशी,
तुम्हारी आकांक्षा है की तुम स्वछंद होकर बहो , मेरी इसका है की ये

स्वछंद धरा मुझे एक पत्थर की भाँती सँवारे , काटे और आकर देती रहे,
इन आकांक्षाओं और इक्छओं के पार भी एक दुनिया है, जहाँ ये
इक्छाएं और आकांक्षाएं एक दुसरे से प्रेम करती हैं,
शायद वहीं हमारा co - dependent प्रेम भी बसर करता है।

तुम्हारी कुछ आकांक्षाएं हैं,
मेरी कुछ इक्छाएं हैं,
पर ये ज़रूरी तो नहीं की इनके बीच हमेशा एक संघर्ष हो ?

14. Small Measure of Peace

Peace is a five-letter word, yet its meanings run deep,
A reminder that brevity does not mean insignificance,
Lessons one should not forget and always keep,
You gather meanings that may not always be relevant,
yet still do not lose their relevance.

I have looked for peace far and wide,
In attempts often rigorous and futile,
At times, looking for it in somebody else's life,
Like a musk deer I have wandered, with peace being my
Kasturi, juggling with wrong and right,
Till the day that I finally met the "You", only to know
that my peace was here, all along in plain sight.

Despite all the heavy meanings and ideas that we may
attribute,
Peace says stop, I do not need your heavily worded
tributes,
Can't you see that I am easy and simple?
You can find me in something as easy as a smile that
brings to life, a dimple.

Peace is a five-letter word, yet its meanings run deep,
It is in something as simple as watching you peacefully

sleep,
It is also in the pride that I take in you for fighting it out despite what hurdles may creep,
Peace is something that I find in myself when I look at your eyes and see that you feel loved,
Peace also finds me when you no more question whether "all your love, is it something that I have deserved?",
Peace also emanates when it is the kid underneath us that enjoys and breathes in our space, safely exposed,
Disappeared I have been for long, only with you I have truly felt seen and heard,
How do I give up on a love like that, despite whatever difficulties life may breed?

Peace is a five-letter word, and yet its meanings run deep,
Though its meanings are deep, its substance remains simple,
We run after complicated meanings while ignoring ever-present simple answers,
I know you will tell me that "do not find peace in someone else",
But then my peace is mine and yours is yours, and you are not merely someone else.

In a world where chaos is in abundance and peace is scant,

One rarely finds his/her small measure of peace in a life that is both short as well as vast,
But once and if you find it, you don't strangle it, but you hold on to it real tight,
For it is worth every obstacle, every test, it is worth every fight.

Peace is a five-letter word, yet its meanings run deep,
Mostly it is in simple things and memories, something which, in the habit of attributing heavy meanings, we forget to cherish and to keep.

15. If you were a city

If you were a city, you would likely be Madras,
Not just because both of you have class, are sizzling hot and have some sass,
It is difficult to truly fall in love with both of you at first sight,
You both need that time and effort to be truly understood and then be loved,
But isn't that the basis of everything substantial, right?

Just like Madras, the real you is held deep within you, real tight,
It is not like you are caging yourselves, but then both of you have protected yourselves against the world, never giving up the good fight ,
One can neither love you both nor understand you with the approach of fright or flight,
On the surface, both of you might appear at times not so welcoming and hostile,
But then your real self is not meant for everyone, especially not those who consider efforts to be futile,
It is all about winning both of your trust, something that needs love, patience, and time.

You are much like the Adyar, you know,

You both knew once upon a time what it means to freely flow,
But then, with time and things, both of you have consciously contained that flow and gone slow,
Though the moment both of you get that safe space and love, your flow does not know how to stem or bow,
I am not lying, for when loved the way you should be, I have seen both you and the Adyar glow.

तुम मद्रास के उन आषाढ़ की बादलों के जैसी हो,
जिनके अंदर बरसात और बरसने की इच्छा तो प्रबल होती है,
पर ना जाने क्यों वो बरस नहीं पाते,
शायद उन्हें भी नहीं पता की क्यों खुद को रोके रखते हैं बरसने से,
कुछ दिनों पर तुम कुछ कुछ मद्रास की बारिश सरीखी भी हो,
जो या तो बरसती ही नहीं , या फिर जब बरसती है तो बस रूकती ही नहीं।

कई दिनों पे तुम मद्रास की हर भोर की धुप भी हो,
जो रौशनी तो लाती ही और साथ साथ एक वार्मथ भी देती है,
कई शामों में शाम के वो ठंढी हवा हो ,
जो मेरी सारी नाकामियों, हताशा और निराशा को मिटा देती है,
जैसे की वो कभी थी ही नहीं।

Your eyes on your pretty face are like Madras harboured by the sea,
They both are deep, unfathomable, and beautiful, not for everyone to see,

You have so many stories buried deep within you, just
like the treasure trove of your stories, which is the sea,
There is so much of Madras in you, and Madras has so
much of you, can't both of you see?

Madras, and you have so much goodness in you despite
all scars,
I conjure similarities between you every time I am sitting
at Elliot, gazing at the stars,
Both of you have character and the sense of originality
that you retain,
After all the waiting and patience, how can I not love
you both and yet refrain?
If you were a city, you would be Madras,
Not just because both of you have class, are sizzling hot,
and have some sass.

16. पोस्टकार्ड ......

आज फिर दराज़ से एक पोस्टकार्ड निकल आया है,
तुम्हारी और तुम्हारी उन आँखों की याद साथ लाया है,
अचानक फिर से हाथों ने कलम की ओर हाथ बढ़ाया है,
लेकिन लिखूं या ना लिखूं उस खाली सी जगह पर,
इस हिचकिचाहट से ना जाने क्यों , पर ज़रा सा मन घबराया है।

सोचा की किसी और को ही लिख लूँ ,
पर फिर कलम और पोस्टकार्ड की कोरी जगह ने ये कहा है,
की शब्द अगर तुम्हारे लिए निकले तो ही मैं लिखूं,
की अगर पोस्टकार्ड पे अपनी बच्चों वाली पेंटिंग करूँ तो बस तुम्हारे लिए करूँ,
वरना पोस्टकार्ड की उस खाली जगह पर मेरे लिया रखा क्या है ?
तुम हो इन अक्षरों में तो कविता है,
तुम हो तो ये दुनिया, दुनिया है,
तुम्हारे सिवा किसी कोई और कविता मैं क्या लिखूं ?
तुम्हारे सिवा मेरे अल्फ़ाज़ों में रखा क्या है ?

उन्हीं दराज़ों से झांकते हुए मुझे पेंटब्रश ने भी चिढ़ाया है,
उठाते ही पेंटब्रश कमरे में पड़ी उस कैनवास ने भी फिर बुलाया है,
पेंटब्रश और कैनवास ने कहा है की फिर से तेरी तस्वीर बनाऊं मैं,
उन दोनों ने बस और बस तुम्हें अपना बनाया है,
रंगों से क्या सजाऊँ तुम्हें मैं,
जबकि तुमने ही ज़िन्दगीको को रंगों का मतलब समझाया है।

आज फिर दराज़ से एक पोस्टकार्ड निकल आया है,
तुम्हारी और तुम्हारी उन आँखों की याद साथ लाया है.......

17. Ocean of Life

Of all the things that I love in this world,
It is your deep, mesmerising eyes that I love the most,
Those bewitching eyes speak of a thousand things,
I just sit in bewilderment and imagine what secrets lie hidden in them.

Amid a hot, lifeless desert,
Just as an oasis is a celebration of life,
So are your eyes an oasis in my life,
For whenever I have been hit and knocked down by life,
It is this oasis that has always motivated me to face those punches with my chin up.

Your eyes tell a thousand untold tales,
They glow like twinkling stars, and I would love to be drowned in their intensity forever.
It stimulates myriad memories that leave an everlasting imprint on me,
This beholder of yours considers himself lucky enough,
To have experienced its warmth when Cupid's arrow strikes.

The whole universe seems enshrined in divine light,
Whenever I look into your eyes,

Time pauses, and the world behind me passes into
oblivion,
I'm often submerged in my own world of thoughts,
Thinking whether I will have its acquaintance ever again
in my life,
I just have this one wish which I hope god may fulfil,
That is to be the chronicler of those stories that your
eyes protect and behold.

18. हताशा की हताशा

मैं तुमसे ये हरगिज़ नहीं कहूंगा की निराश मत होना,
जिस प्रकार मेहनत तुम्हारी है, निराशा भी तुम्हारी है,
लेकिन इन निराशा के बादलों के बीच ये कभी मत भूलना,
की ये जो रास्ता तुमने तय किया है, इसे भी तुमने ही हर चट्टान को काट कर बनाया है,
जिस खून ने सींचा है इस सफर को, उसी भी तो तुम्हारी धमनियों ने ही बहाया है।

चलो पता है मुझे मैं अक्सर तुम्हें कुछ बातें नहीं बतलाता हूँ,
आज तुम्हें ना हरा पाने वाली तुम्हारी हताशा के साथ अपनी मुलाकात की कहानी सुनाता हूँ,
एक दिन हताशा मेरे बगल मैं बैठ गयी हताश होकर,
हताशा मुझे नहीं जानती थी, पर मैं पहचानता था की वो तुम्हारी है,
ठीक वैसे ही जैसे मैं पहचानता हूँ हर उस चीज़ को जो तुम्हारी है,
मैंने हाथ बढ़ाया और कहा की चलो कुछ दूर चलते हैं,
वो उठी और मेरे साथ चलने लगी धीऱे धीऱे ।

मैंने पुछा की हताशा तुम हताश क्यों हो ?
उसने कहा की आखिर क्यों ना हूँ मैं हताश ?
फिर उसने बताया की वो तुम्हारी हताशा है,
कहा की निराश तो कर देती हूँ उसे, पर हमेशा की लिए हताश नहीं कर पाती,
फिर पुछा उसने मुझसे की आखिर करूँ तो मैं क्या करूँ ?

मैंने कहाँ की कुछ मत करो, तुम कुछ कर भी नहीं सकती हो ,
क्यूंकि वो अड़ी है, अपने सपनों की लिए हमेशा लड़ी है,
रुकी है अक्सर अपने सफर में, थमी कभी नहीं है,
थकी है कई शामों में, लेकिन झुकी कभी नहीं है,
आँधियाँ आयी हैं उसके सफर में उसे तोड़ने की मंशा से,
विचित्र थेथर है वो, देखो अब भी पूरी शक्ति से खड़ी है,
हताशा तुम हारी ही हो उससे, अपने वजूद के बारे में सोचो, क्यों अब भी जीत की मिथ्या में पड़ी हो।

चलते चलते हम दोनों सीवान तक आ पहुंचे,
हताशा मुड़ी और मुझसे बोली की ठीक है अब मैं जाती हूँ ,
अपने प्रेमी, निराशा को भी ये बात समझती हूँ,
की वो परेशान तो कर सकता है, पर हरा नहीं सकता इस औरत को,
कैसे जीतेंगे हम जहाँ इतनी लगन, इक्छाशक्ति और गैरत हो।

मैं तुमसे ये हरगिज़ नहीं कहूंगा की निराश मत होना,
जिस प्रकार मेहनत तुम्हारी है, निराशा भी तुम्हारी है,
लेकिन इन निराशा के बादलों के बीच ये कभी मत भूलना,
की मंज़िल जो तुम्हारे लिए इंतज़ार कर रही है, वो भी सिर्फ तुम्हारी और बस तुम्हारी है।

19. मैं कुछ और जीना चाहता हूँ.......

मैं कुछ और जीना चाहता हूँ,
तुम्हें सच में खुश देखना चाहता हूँ,
तुम्हारी भीतर वो जो मासूम सा बच्चा है उसकी खिलखिलाहट सुनना चाहता हूँ,
तुम्हें चहचहाते हुए मेहसूस करना चाहता हूँ,
हाँ, मैं कुछ और जीना चाहता हूँ।

और मैं हर चौथे शनिवार की तरह,
हमेशा उस लोहे के दरवाज़े के पार तुम्हारा इंतज़ार करना चाहता हूँ,
तुम्हारा इंतज़ार करना शायद मेरी सबसे प्यारी आदत है,
ऐसी आदत की जब तुमसे मिलने की कोई उम्मीद न हो, तब भी वही खड़ा रहूँ ,
शायद बिना उम्मीद के भी इंतज़ार करने में ही सच्ची शिद्दत है,
हो सकता है एक दिन तुम निकलो वहां से और मुझे ना देखो,
पर जिस दिन सच में खुश हो कर निकलो वहां से, बस मुस्कुरा देना,
तुम शायद मुझे ना देख पाओ, पर मैं उस हँसी को देख लूँगा।

मैं कुछ और जीना चाहता हूँ,
उस दिन तक तो साँसें लेना चाहता हूँ,
हो सकता है इसके बाद भी मेरी जान मुझ में रेह जाए,
उसके बाद, अगर हो सके तो मैं तुम्हारे जीना चाहता हूँ,
पर उस दिन तक मैं कुछ और जीना चाहता हूँ.....

20. प्रेम

सारे दुःख, झगड़ों , निराशा के बाद,
अंत में जो बच जाता है ,
जिससे हृदय कुंठित नहीं महसूस करता,
शायद वही सच्चा प्रेम है।

www.ingramcontent.com/pod-product-compliance
Lightning Source LLC
LaVergne TN
LVHW050820051026
849532LV00008B/3046